LET'S FIND OUT! GOVERNMENT
D0125022
WHAT IS CITIZENSHIP?
LAURA LORIA
Britannica
Educational Publishing
IN ASSOCIATION WITH
ROSEN
EDUCATIONAL SERVICES

Published in 2016 by Britannica Educational Publishing (a trademark of Encyclopædia Britannica, Inc.) in association with The Rosen Publishing Group, Inc.
29 East 21st Street, New York, NY 10010

Distributed exclusively by Rosen Publishing.
To see additional Britannica Educational Publishing titles, go to rosenpublishing.com.

First Edition

Britannica Educational Publishing
J. E. Luebering: Director, Core Reference Group
Mary Rose McCudden: Editor, Britannica Student Encyclopedia

Rosen Publishing
Hope Lourie Killcoyne: Executive Editor
Heather Moore Niver: Editor
Nelson Sá: Art Director
Nicole Russo: Designer
Cindy Reiman: Photography Manager

Library of Congress Cataloging-in-Publication Data

Loria, Laura.
What is citizenship?/Laura Loria.—First Edition.
pages cm.—(Let's find out! Government)
Includes bibliographical references and index.
ISBN 978-1-62275-976-7 (library bound)—ISBN 978-1-62275-977-4 (pbk.)—
ISBN 978-1-62275-979-8 (6-pack)
1. Citizenship—United States—Juvenile literature. 2. Civics—Juvenile literature. I. Title.
JK1759.L75 2015
323.60973—dc23

2014037266

Manufactured in the United States of America

Photo credits: Cover, p. 1 Scott Olson/Getty Images; p. 4 Mike Watson Images/moodboard/Thinkstock; p. 5 Muriel de Seze/Digital Vision/Getty Images; p. 6 bikeriderlondon/Shutterstock.com; p. 7 Creatista/Shutterstock.com; p. 8 S. Borisov/Shutterstock.com; pp. 9 Blend Images – Hill Street Studios/Brand X Pictures/Getty Images; pp. 10, 13, 14, 15, 16 © AP Images; p. 11 Timothy A. Clary/AFP/Getty Images; p. 12 NARA; p. 17 Stockbyte/Thinkstock; p. 18 Sgt. Benjamin E. Woodle/U.S. Marines Corps Photo; p. 19 Private Collection/Peter Newark American Pictures/Bridgeman Images; p. 20 John Elk III/Lonely Planet Images/Getty Images; p. 21 Stock Montage/Archive Photos/Getty Images; p. 22 Woods Wheatcroft/Aurora/Getty Images; p. 23 jim kruger/E+/Getty Images; p. 24 Betsie Van Der Meer/Taxi/Getty Images; p. 25 Jonathan Rashad/Moment/Getty Images; p. 26 Ryan/Beyer/The Image Bank/Getty Images; p. 27 Jed Jacobsohn/Sports Illustrated/Getty Images; p. 28 Blend Images – KidStock/Brand X Pictures/Getty Images; p. 29 Jewel Samad/AFP/Getty Images; interior pages background image Instinia/Shutterstock.com

Contents

Members of a Country

Members of a club or team follow rules, care for others, and work together. Other group members help them reach their goals. They all feel like they are a part of something important.

A citizen is a full member of a country. People may live in a country without being a citizen. They may move to a country for a job or to be with family. In some cases they will leave after a few years. But most people who live in

Any team must cooperate to achieve a goal, such as winning a championship. Championship teams win because they help each other.

Think About It

A citizen is a member of a country. What would it be like to live in a country if you were not a citizen?

a country are full citizens of that country.

Citizens have rights that are given by the country's government. For example, citizens have the right to be protected by a country's laws. In return, citizens have duties that they owe to the country. One of the most important duties is being loyal to the country. People can lose their citizenship if they do not fulfill their duties.

When people move to another country, they try to learn where important places are located. This way, they know where to go to get the things they need or where to get help.

Who Is a Citizen?

In the United States, anyone who is born here is a citizen, even if his or her parents are not citizens.

Most countries have three basic ways for someone to become a citizen. First, and simplest, anyone born in the country is a citizen of that country.

Second, anyone whose parent is a citizen of the country is also a citizen. For example, if a U.S. citizen gives birth to a baby in another country, then that baby is considered a citizen of the United States. This is called acquired citizenship.

The third way is by going through a process called naturalization. Naturalization is a way for people who are born in one country to become citizens of another country. Laws on naturalization are different from country to country. Often the person must be a permanent resident of the country for several years, must pass a test proving that he or she knows the laws and history of the country, and must take an **oath** of loyalty to the country.

VOCABULARY
An **oath** is a serious promise.

Children born to U.S. citizens are also given citizenship, even when they are born in other parts of the world.

Becoming a Naturalized Citizen

Today, more than 600,000 people are naturalized in the United States each year. Naturalization is a long and difficult process. Candidates must live in the country for five years. Candidates who are married to U.S. citizens can apply for citizenship after three years

The Statue of Liberty has welcomed millions of people to the United States, many of whom wish to become citizens.

Think About It

In the 1970s, immigrants made up about 5 percent of the U.S. population, or number of people living in the United States. Today, they make up about 13 percent. Why do you think that number has increased?

of living in the country. After they apply for citizenship, candidates cannot move out of the country for any period of time. They must be able to read, write, and speak the English language.

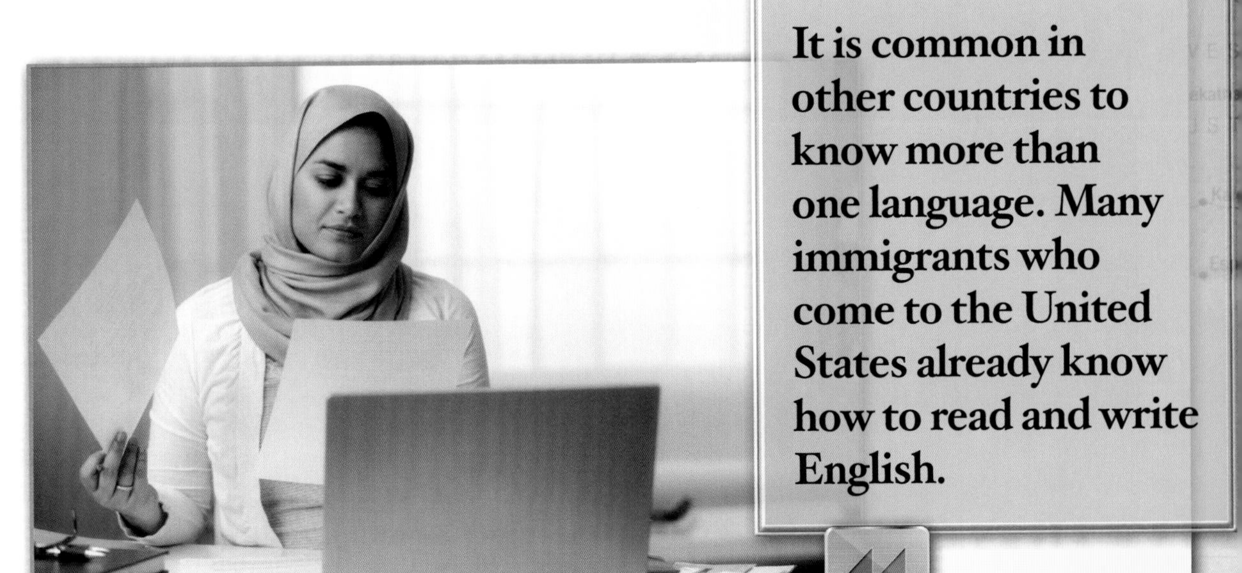

It is common in other countries to know more than one language. Many immigrants who come to the United States already know how to read and write English.

People who want to become U.S. citizens take a test about the country's laws and history. Candidates are asked 10 out of a possible 100 questions. The candidate must answer six correctly. Older people, who have lived in the United States for a long time, may be allowed to take the test in a language other than English.

People who want to become naturalized often take classes in citizenship. They study hard to be able to pass the test.

Candidates who pass the test take part in a ceremony. They promise to be loyal to the United States, support the laws of the country, and defend the country from enemies. After taking the citizenship oath, the candidate is a full U.S. citizen. Not every country allows immigrants to become naturalized citizens.

COMPARE AND CONTRAST

How is being a naturalized citizen more difficult than being a citizen by birth?

People from all over the world become American citizens at a naturalization ceremony. Their families and friends come to see them take their oaths.

Citizens' Rights

In the United States the basic law of the country is called the Constitution. Soon after it was written, the country's leaders added the Bill of Rights. The Bill of Rights explains the basic freedoms and rights of all citizens of the country.

Citizens of the United States have freedom of speech and press. The government cannot prevent them from saying, writing, or thinking whatever

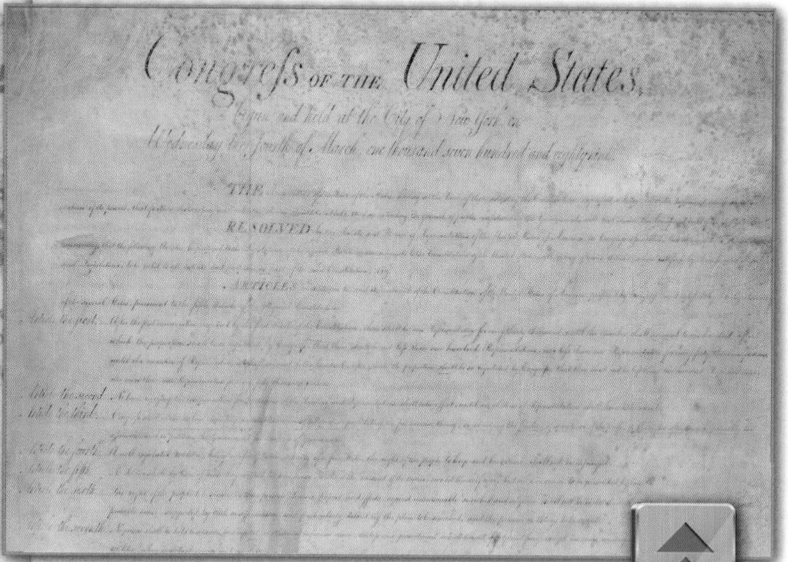

The original Bill of Rights can be found in the National Archives in Washington, D.C., the capital of the United States of America.

The freedoms of speech and press allow people to disagree with the government and try to change it by sharing their opinions and ideas.

they want. In general citizens have the freedom to say whatever they want, in whatever form.

Citizens must be reasonable in their speech, though. For example, you cannot yell "fire" in a crowded theater unless there's really a fire. Also, you cannot speak, write, or draw something false that injures someone's good name.

Citizens also have the freedom of assembly and the freedom of religion. They may gather in peaceful groups and they may practice any religion they choose.

The government also provides some

In the United States, citizens may practice any religion they choose or none at all. The government cannot tell people which religion they must follow.

Think About It

How would the United States be different if people were not guaranteed rights? Would you want to be a citizen?

A judge watches over a trial to make sure that the accused person's rights are protected. The judge helps everyone follow the rules in court.

protections for its citizens. These include the right to fair treatment by the government. Citizens have the right to privacy. Part of this right means that the police cannot come into citizens' homes unless they have a reason to think the citizens are breaking a law.

Vocabulary

An **accused** person is blamed for doing something. It does not mean that the person is guilty.

Citizens **accused** of breaking a law still have many rights. They have a right to a fair trial, meaning the government must prove that they are guilty. If a citizen is guilty of a crime, the punishment must be fair.

Citizens' Responsibilities

Voting is a citizen's duty, or responsibility. It is also a right. Citizens vote to make sure that the government is run well and that it works for the good of its citizens. Every U.S. citizen's vote is equal. Some people choose not to vote, but they lose a chance to have a say in their government.

Citizens age 18 or older, who have not committed serious crimes, have the right to vote. Their votes are secret to protect people's privacy.

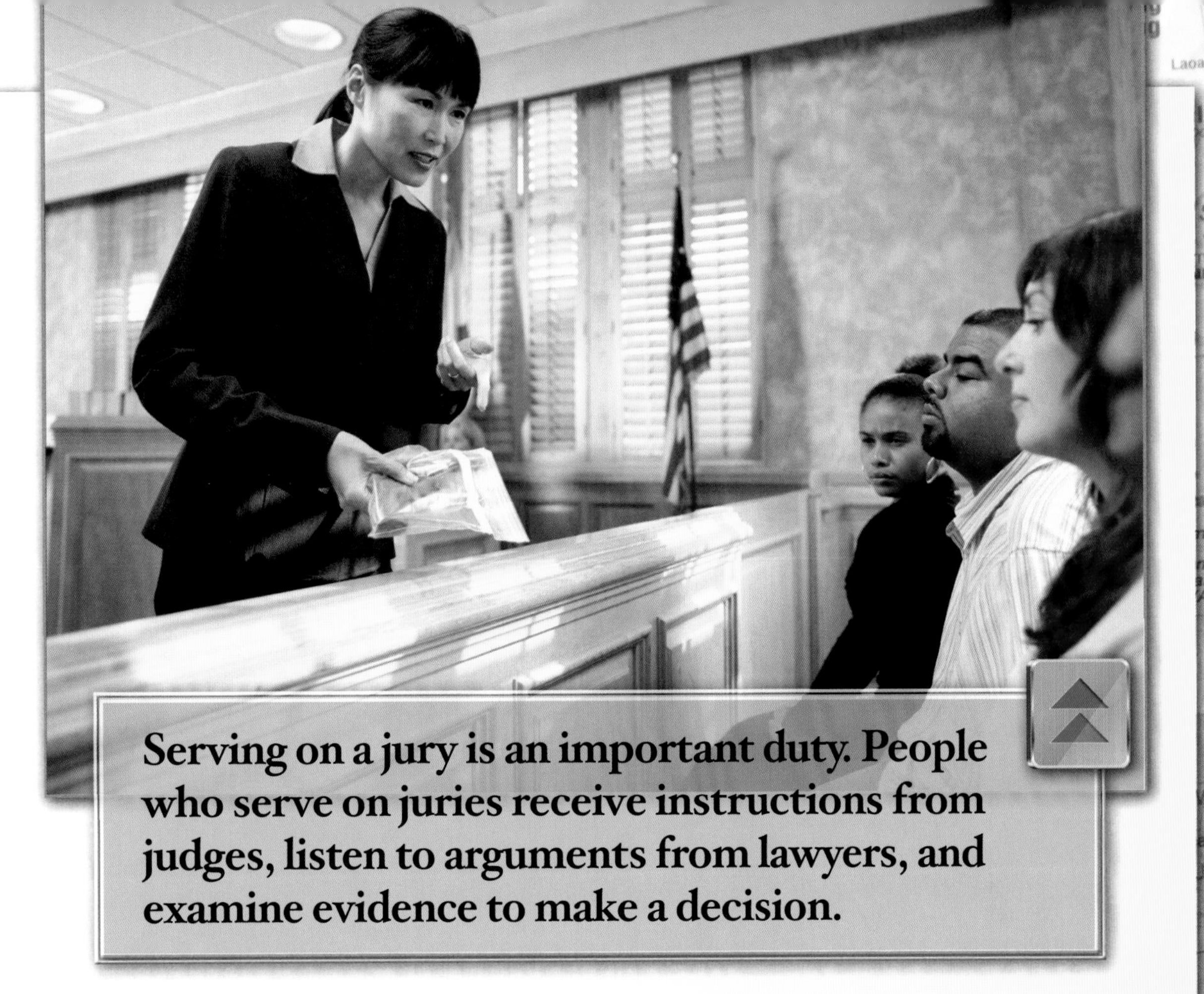

Serving on a jury is an important duty. People who serve on juries receive instructions from judges, listen to arguments from lawyers, and examine evidence to make a decision.

Citizens are required by law to serve on a jury if they are asked to. A jury is a group of people who hear a case in court and decide whether a person is innocent or guilty. In most cases, citizens accused of crimes are guaranteed a trial by a jury of their peers, or other citizens. This helps keep our courts fair for everyone.

Citizens must be prepared to defend their country by serving in the military. Joining the army or other branch of the armed forces is usually **voluntary**. Sometimes if the U.S. military needs more

VOCABULARY
Something is **voluntary** if people choose to do it on their own.

The men and women who join the armed forces must be physically fit to protect the citizens of the United States.

COMPARE AND CONTRAST
Are rights or responsibilities more important for citizens?

members, it can draft people to join and fight. Today, only men are required to serve if necessary, but women may have this responsibility in the future.

If citizens do not fulfill their responsibilities, they can lose their citizenship. However, this is very rare. If a citizen of the United States tries to overthrow the government by force, becomes a citizen of another country, or joins the military of another country, the government can take away citizenship. A person with no citizenship is called stateless.

Even a powerful citizen, like former vice president Aaron Burr, could lose his citizenship if he were to commit treason, a crime against the country. Burr was accused of treason in 1807, but he was found not guilty.

Citizens Are Caring

A citizen cares for others by making sure that their rights aren't ignored. All citizens have rights and all citizens' rights are equal. For example, the right to free speech applies to everyone. This means that citizens should allow everyone to share their ideas. They should

Taxes paid by citizens are used for public services, such as this park. Citizens pay for things like this, which are good for the whole community.

Think About It

Is a citizen free to do whatever he or she wants? When should a person think about the rights of other people?

respect the right of everyone to speak, not just protect their own right.

Citizens must also think about others' needs. People have different needs, and the government works to try to meet as many needs as it can. Citizens help the government achieve this by paying taxes, even if it means paying for things they disagree with or don't need for themselves. U.S. President Theodore Roosevelt said, "This country will not permanently be a good place for any of us to live in unless we make it a reasonably good place for all of us to live in."

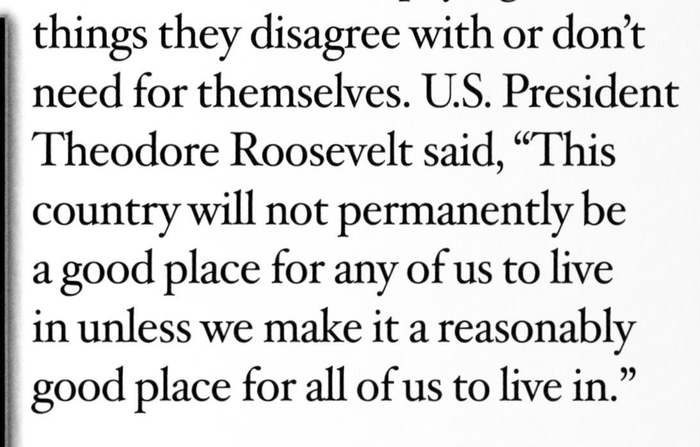

President Theodore Roosevelt believed that good citizens must be very active in their governments.

Citizens Are Responsible

Good citizens take responsibility for their own actions. Obeying laws is one way to be responsible. When citizens follow laws, they help create a country in which people can enjoy their freedoms without fear. Citizens depend on one another to control themselves and their actions.

Obeying traffic laws helps keep drivers, passengers, bicyclists, and walkers safe. Sharing the road is one way to be responsible for everyone's safety.

Think About It

Can a country be successful if its citizens are not responsible?

Good citizens also tell the truth to make sure that all people are treated fairly. When citizens speak in a court during a trial, they must swear to tell the truth. When citizens are honest, they can trust one another.

Citizens should use good judgment. Laws help citizens to keep peace, but people must think for themselves about what is right or wrong. Good judgment is also important when voting.

Promising to tell the truth is very serious. If a person lies in court, he or she can be charged with a crime and could go to jail.

Citizens Are Respectful

The United States is made up of people from many different places with many different ideas and traditions. Citizens of the United States are respectful of one another. That means that they listen to everyone, even if they do not agree with them. They defend everyone's right to have their own opinions.

Unfortunately, people in America have often been

Citizens may have differences, but they have many things in common as well. They are all a part of the same country and have the same rights and responsibilities.

These citizens of Egypt are protesting their government. In the United States, protests like this have helped to change unfair laws.

treated unfairly because of their race, gender, religion, or national origin. The Civil Rights Act of 1964 says that treating people poorly because of these differences is wrong. The law was created because many citizens protested about unfair treatment.

Compare and Contrast

U.S. citizens have the right to protest, but protesting is against the law in some countries. How is protest good for a country?

Citizens Are Patriotic

There are many ways for citizens to be patriotic and to show their love for their country. Patriotism can give people a sense of belonging to a national community. It should not make people think that their country or group is better than any other.

One way to be patriotic is to fly the country's flag. Another way to show patriotic spirit is through

Fireworks displays are held on the Fourth of July across the country to celebrate the birth of our nation.

sporting events and other worldwide competitions. The Olympic Games, held every two years, are a collection of international athletic contests. Athletes from all over the United States compete against athletes from other countries. Winning medals at the Olympics is a source of pride for the athletes because they represent their country at the games.

Skier Mikaela Shiffrin won a gold medal for the United States at the 2014 Winter Olympics in Sochi, Russia.

Think About It

What are some patriotic symbols or actions you see in your community?

You Are a Citizen

Most rights and responsibilities of citizens are for adults, but children are citizens, too. Young people show their citizenship by following rules, just as adults follow laws. They respect other students and their teachers, just as adult citizens respect their neighbors and government officials.

Children are also citizens of their community. They can **participate** in community activities, such as clubs or volunteer organizations. They can also get to know community

Volunteering is a great way to help your community. Good citizens work together to make their country a better place to live.

leaders, such as police officers and librarians. Communicating with leaders is one way children can participate in their community.

VOCABULARY
To **participate** means to take part in an activity.

Young people can prepare for their lives as citizens of the United States in many ways. You can learn about American history. You can also read the newspaper to learn about what's going on in your country and in your government.

Not all citizens will get to meet the president of the United States, but there are opportunities to meet with other community leaders at school and in your town.

GLOSSARY

acquire To come into possession of; to gain.

assembly A group of persons gathered together.

candidate One who wants to be elected to an office or to be accepted for a position.

communities Groups of people with common interests.

defend To keep safe from danger or attack.

draft Forced military service.

guarantee Promise to do, make, or keep.

judgment A decision made after thinking carefully.

jury A group of people who must judge something or someone.

naturalization The process of becoming a citizen.

patriotic Having pride in one's country.

protest Object or complain.

right Something to which one has a fair claim.

society A group of people who have common traditions, institutions, and interests.

stateless Without citizenship.

tolerance Accepting other peoples' different feelings, habits, or beliefs.

unique The only one of its kind.

For More Information

Books

Bamaton, Paul. *Elections: Choosing Our Leaders* (Explore Citizenship). New York, NY: PowerKids Press, 2009.

Leavitt, Amie Jane. *The Bill of Rights in Translation: What It Really Means.* Mankato, MN: Coughlan Press, 2008.

Maury, Rob. *Citizenship: Rights and Responsibilities.* Philadelphia, PA: Manson Crest Publishers, 2009.

Raum, Elizabeth. *The Pledge of Allegiance in Translation: What It Really Means.* Mankato, MN: Coughlan Press, 2008.

Sobel, Sly. *The U.S. Constitution and You*. Hauppage, NY: Barron's, 2012.

Websites

Because of the changing nature of Internet links, Rosen Publishing has developed an online list of websites related to the subject of this book. This site is updated regularly. Please use this link to access this list:

http://www.rosenlinks.com/LFO/Citi

Index